A Book of hours

226

AUTO-Apocrypha

misTruths — half Lies —

— an anecdotal personal history orally Transmitted.

The things i believe — or — ??

The WEIRD stories about me (as a baby).

The family; the world, god, the flesh, & the devil — everything else

That they told me when I was

a kid & believed everything —
absolutely uncritically

Anecdoubts — sore sure

Anecdoubts SURE

Anecdoubts

chronical of dubiously acquired personal history

unsure semi-false

quasi-possible

Autopocrypha —

anecdoubts.

Book of DOUBTS   zapsday diary

Anecdoubtful →   aned   partial

Harrington
STREET

1 Harrington ST —

IT's a one block
STreeT located in
San francisco's
excelsior DisTrict.

ITs a gentle slope
The up side by mission st.
The down side.. by
Akmany blvd.
* historical footnote

My Daddy

Harrington
STREET

J ERRY
Garcia

Delacorte ▤ Press

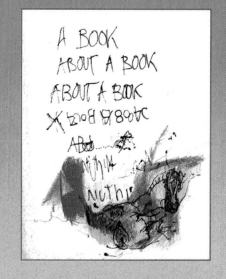

Published by
Delacorte Press
Bantam Doubleday Dell Publishing Group, Inc.
1540 Broadway
New York, New York 10036

ISBN 0-385-31353-5

Manufactured in the United States of America
Published simultaneously in Canada

November 1995

10 9 8 7 6 5 4 3 2 1

A Note from Deborah Garcia

During the years Jerry and I were together, he spent hours and hours telling me stories about San Francisco. It seemed a magical place to me. Jerry, with his winning way with words and his vast knowledge of every odd and basic fact, was the perfect guide to this enchanting city. Of course, it was the stories about his own young life that fascinated me the most. Because of these, and the enormous personal charm he directed my way, Jerry became a figure of romance to me. He was born at midnight, his father was from Spain, he swam in the Sutro Baths, played at Playland, had sea captains, diamond cutters, and musicians in his family.

For the first five years Jerry lived an idyllic life in 1940s San Francisco, old San Francisco: His parents loved each other and all around them was an exciting city, a place where even during the war, people celebrated. But Jerry told me, as his mother had told him, that his birth had been so difficult his father had signed what were then called "dismemberment papers" allowing the doctor to save the mother rather than the baby. Newborn Jerry spent weeks in an incubator. When he was five he saw his father drown in the American River and everything changed. He developed asthma, which was treated then by hospital visits and shots of adrenaline. So a lot of his childhood was spent in bed, drawing. Yet he was a happy child, his aunt Lenore told us, always a smile on his face, always singing. And always drawing.

This lifelong good habit served Jerry well. He was a profoundly industrious person, he loved to work, and his work was his play. If there was paper, he would draw on it, if there was a piano around, he would sit down and play it. When he started work on this book, I remember him walking into the room one day and proudly proclaiming, "I've discovered I'm a writer!" Well, of course you are, I said, having encouraged him in this direction often, you are the most articulate person around. The push toward discovery was highly enjoyable for Jerry, an essential component of his personality and character.

During the eighteen months Jerry composed this book, he worked on it all the time, nearly every day. It had a high fun factor, lots of color, a deadline. He liked certain traditions—"keep the good stuff"—yet he always found, right off, the latest high-tech toys. For the book he drew the original pieces, scanned them into the Mac, and worked up lots of versions. And he could do all this holed up on the road too. Perfect. Like a child's story-book, but very adult. That, too, was Jerry. He was a big kid, with a beard. Of all the ways someone might go back and explore childhood, the one Jerry chose suited him ideally: create a marvelous picture book.

It seemed, as I saw the book develop, that in deciding which stories to choose, exploring various versions in pictures and words, Jerry came to terms with some aspects of his past, reclaiming it, and that the joy he found in the work overpowered the pain of the events themselves. One of the saddest things he told me was that for a year after his father's death, whenever he heard his father's name he would burst out crying. I know now how he felt. Jerry carried his grief with him, as well as his joy, and the line between them was what he drew in his art and in his music: a pure deep line of longing and triumph.

Although Jerry's name has become synonymous with the '60s, he brought to the '60s his own spirit, wild and inventive, and this big generous spirit carried him and so many others along for the next three decades. Always he remained current, an evolving artist rather than an artifact. The world loved him for this.

Jerry's life came full circle: He often told me that these last few years were the happiest of his life. The child who had his family split apart grew into the man who for thirty years created a happy family for millions of people, something they could belong to for the price of a ticket. He loved that. The week before his death, Jerry cheerfully announced to me, "I've discovered I'm an optimist!" And he was. No one should underestimate what a long dark struggle it was for him to arrive at that place. Jerry had become that sweet-faced boy again, full of love and promise. His spirit was strong. He lost the lifelong struggle with his body far too soon, but what a wonderful life he had. This gentle, kind, and talented man gave so much to so many. This book, which came from his heart and helped him heal his heart, is a gift we all can share.

Deborah Koons
Deborah Koons
J Nero 123456789
J J Jerome
Jerome
Garcia

my darling Deborah

Here's how it started:

Somebody (I don't remember who) said, "Hey! why don't you write an autobiography?" It got me thinking... "Let's see... I don't think my life has produced those alpha events like.. D-Day - the Rubicon - the Russian winter you know the kind of stuff that would rate an autobiography!" and I politely declined,.... sort of

However - the inquiries kept pouring in from friends, literary agents, publishers...etc.

& finally the nice people at Dell made me an offer I couldn't refuse!." "Come up with 24 drawings—painting whatever, and a facing page of commentary, dialogue or doggeral, and we will publish — it, post haste." So I set out on a hurried rummage of : through my personal past vainly seeking Big events to write about.

(Oh sure, your thinking

what about the 60's? what about woodstock'?
How's about the real story of the Grateful dead? etc. etc.
Well, I always figured these subjects would be best understood,
by poring over the many accounts (Journalistic, Personal,

historic.) sortof reaching your own conclusions via
gleaning... I've felt that my perspective was necessarily
warped as well as .. pretty much hopelessly subjective..
but.....

This book stuff wouldn't go away! and any way
I'd already embarassed myself with a book of interviews
published in the 70's and a much more recent book of
art that was ~~~~~ ~~~~~ well recieved—sort of
etc.

rearing its ugly head.) I would
tend off most queries
by saying something like..
"hey, I'm waiting for something
to happen or you wanna like
church hill or some one
like that.!"

writers apologia

It goes on in this way
for another page or so

Publisher's Note

We are very glad to say that Jerry Garcia's *Harrington Street* is the book that "wouldn't go away."

After a series of preliminary meetings and discussions in 1993, Jerry's "rummage" through his personal past coalesced around the idea of those formative childhood experiences that assume mythical, talismanic proportions in our memories — the rites of passage, big and small, that we all recall through the fluid, magical lens of childhood and that essentially shape us, for good and ill, for the more strictured adult passages to come. And in keeping with his own outsized life and talents, what a childhood Jerry remembered...

He began work in earnest on *Harrington Street* about eighteen months ago and a steady stream, then a torrent, of words and images cascaded from his house in Marin County and from tour cities across the country. He was exhilarated by the process of exploring a new creative medium and tapping his talents as a writer in a full-fledged book, his first. In an early progress meeting, he described his work:

> It's **AUTO-APOCRYPHA**, full of my **ANECDOUBTS**. Like things to do with my relatives, my family, the block I grew up on, the things that scared me (animals), the discovery of fire, you know, things like that. I've written to age 10. I talk to myself, sort of remember things about my family, things they told me, things I think I heard. Then I wonder how I picked up that information, as it seems so familiar. But then it is twisted through my own imagination, which is warped. I write the text out longhand, but my drawings, which illustrate my text, I do on computer. I'm taking it totally freely, it's really FUN! I'm pleased with what I am doing. The look is so unique — it doesn't look like anything else I have ever seen!!!

Last January, Jerry and Dell president and publisher Carole Baron outlined the basic contents and structure of the book, and they chose the title *Harrington Street*, a reference to 87 Harrington Street in San Francisco, where he lived from age five on with his maternal grandparents following his father's tragic death. At other meetings along the way Jerry meticulously selected the final size for the book, the paper, and the typeface, and discussed his plans for the overall look of each page and for the jacket. In a week-long working session last June with Delacorte editor Tracy Devine, he delivered much of the text and art for the book, and they identified the remaining work to be done.

When Jerry died on August 9, 1995, with the completion of *Harrington Street* in sight, he left pages and pages of handwritten notes and typeset text, sketches, drawings, calligraphy, and enough MBs of computer art to fry several serious hard drives (which, in fact, he did, in the course of working on this book). And he left his indelible enthusiasm and vision for the book, for us to finish in accordance with his plans.

Almost everything in these pages is Jerry Garcia's — his words, his art, his creation. In all but two cases, we had Jerry's actual writing for each story. In some instances he had written several slightly different versions or amplifications of a story, and we've tried to include as much as possible here — some versions handwritten, others typeset as he had wished. All typeset text has been read carefully against Jerry's original handwritten text for accuracy and nuance. For the two stories for which he had not yet written text, we pooled our memories of his dazzling verbal renditions with those of Deborah Garcia, and have supplied a simple third-person narrative that strives to recapture the spirit and words Jerry himself would have used. These third-person narratives are set in italics to further distinguish them from Jerry's own first-person text.

In sitting down to sort through Jerry's enormous cache of material to make final selections for the book we replicated a process we were scheduled to undertake with him last August. As it stands, given his crystal-clear intentions, our extensive discussions with him, and invaluable consultations with Deborah, we feel confident that *Harrington Street* reflects the final look and feel Jerry was shooting for. He wanted every page to be different, exciting, full of surprises; and he felt that the book need not follow a strict chronology but should rather evoke the heady, teeming world of childhood for every reader. Our designer, Robin Arzt, who also met with Jerry from the beginning, has faithfully used Jerry's own images, words, and colors to achieve his vision. And even given the sad and daunting task of working on without Jerry, it's been a strange and magical collaboration for us all: Whenever we felt stymied or at an impasse, the perfect piece, the right words, would surface in one of our files. It was all there for us, from Jerry, and the book seemed to come together almost by itself under our hands. We hope that it is not too presumptuous to say that we each felt him guiding us at every step along the way, because it's true.

Harrington Street might never have been launched at all without that kind of magical collaboration, the magic Jerry Garcia specialized in. It was friendship, finally, that brought Jerry to Delacorte Press to begin with. Enormous thanks are due to Hal Kant, Jerry's longtime legal adviser and general counsel to the Grateful Dead, who first suggested the key combination of paintings and drawings and words together as the perfect format for a Jerry Garcia book, and who steadfastly shepherded the book past every possible pitfall, and to Sandra Ruch, facilitator extraordinaire, who was also present at the creation and who kept things moving, especially at the critical early stages. Both Hal and Sandra happen to be old friends of Carole Baron's, and we believe those kinds of personal connections made a difference to Jerry, and to the project. David Raffarin and Tom Paddock of SRA Engineering kept the computers humming for Jerry, and for us. Our technical wizard, Brenden Hitt, worked to make every spread pixel-perfect. Mary Fischer, our production director, and her superb team of suppliers miraculously made an impossible production schedule possible. And without Robin Arzt's brilliant management of the creative and technical complexities of *Harrington Street*, the book would never have become a reality. Finally, we will never be able to fully express our appreciation to Deborah Koons Garcia, who in the midst of her own personal tragedy marshaled the courage and grace to see her husband's work through to its proper completion. She encouraged Jerry in his writing and made important suggestions to him throughout his work on the book, and after his death she gave us all the assistance we asked for and more. Her acute eye and comments added the necessary final polish.

As for ourselves, we feel profoundly privileged to have walked with Jerry along Harrington Street far enough to be able to bring his sights and sounds to you.

New York City
November 1995

early words

Cap'n Olsen.
HERE Kitty.
Swimming lesson
fire !!
Girls up the street
Tillio & Bill

1. BORN — mom told me!
2. Early Memories — Visions
3. Religion — 121 Amazon
4. DADDY — (DEATH)
5. Aftermath — aftermath!?
6. GIRLS — kid sex
7. Nana & Pop — mamma & papa wella (La abuela)
87 HARRINGTON — Radio & TV.
the block — grammar school
8. Tiff.
9. Larger family
10.
11. The guys — The Bar — St. Louis
12. school Teachers — Miss Simon
    peninsula — Mr Carver
    pre adolesc.

My brother Tiff and I lived with our maternal grandparents, Bill and Tillie Clifford, aka "Pop" and "Nana"... or "Nan" for short, in a small white stucco-front, two-story house on Harrington Street in the Excelsior district of San Francisco.

This arrangement began during the devastating emotional aftermath of my father's accidental death by drowning in 1947.

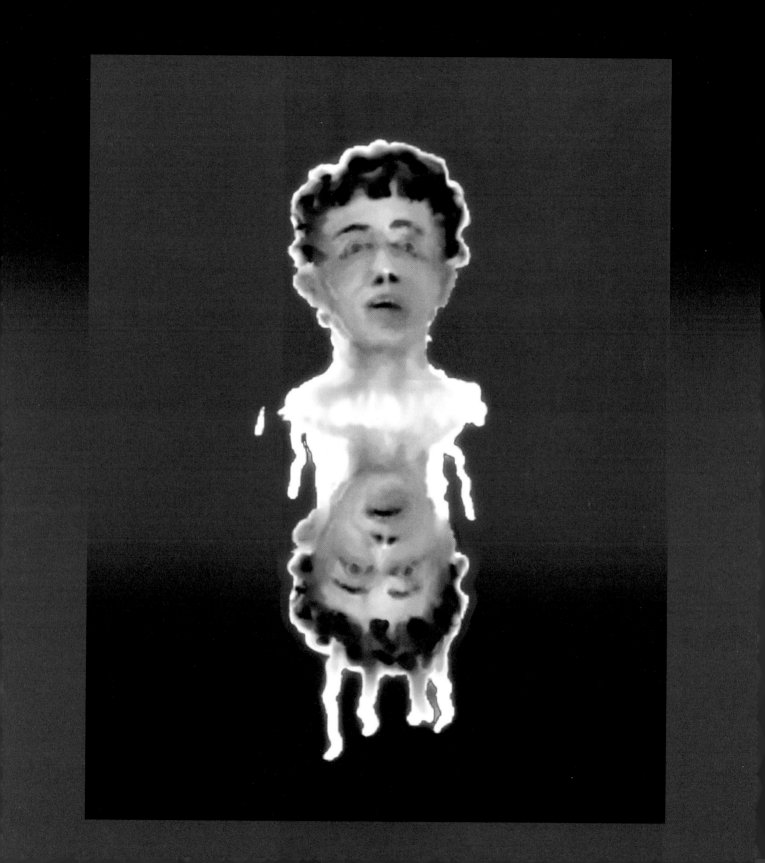

Tillie & Bill - Nan & pop.
My mom's parents (my grand parents)

Bill Clifford and Tillie Olsen were an odd couple… I mean *really* odd. As a kid, of course, I found no contradiction in their relationship (I didn't notice any). It's only with the so-called sophistication of adulthood that some of the more bizarre details stand out as being possibly the least bit unconventional.

A large part of the "oddness" I referred to seemed to be an enormous mismatch of personality types…

enormous differences in personality, style and energy, differences so vast that I, at any rate, am totally unable to imagine what could have attracted them to each other in the first place.

They never talked about each other, much less reminisced about their courtship. In fact, I don't really remember them talking to each other at all.

her name was
in the paper.
and, once in a while,
so was her picture
and at family
gatherings. My Auntie
Ruth, the family
Spielmeister
would unwind
dozens of witty
stories
about Nan.

NAN

Loved Hawaii
universal love
outgoing
political
genuine.
lightly Philosophical
immensely popular.
smart
Hard working
sassy
loyal - Hard Headed -

Tillie Clifford,
My Grand moth
my Mom mom
"Nana": when we we
little kids, "Nan",
older & grown ups,
was the super star
of the family. She wo
a legitimate celebrit
a politician, She was
the Secretary-treasurer
of the laundry workers
union, an elected post.

She was a handsome woman, and probably had been a beautiful girl, at least that was what my brother and I believed when we were kids and lived with our grandparents, Bill and Tillie Clifford.

Our bedroom boasted a large, nicely framed antique sepia portrait of a lovely woman with long black hair piled up on her head Gibson Girl style, and smoldering dark eyes. We were convinced this beauty was, in fact, Tillie our grandmother/aka Nana or "Nan" for short, when she was a girl.

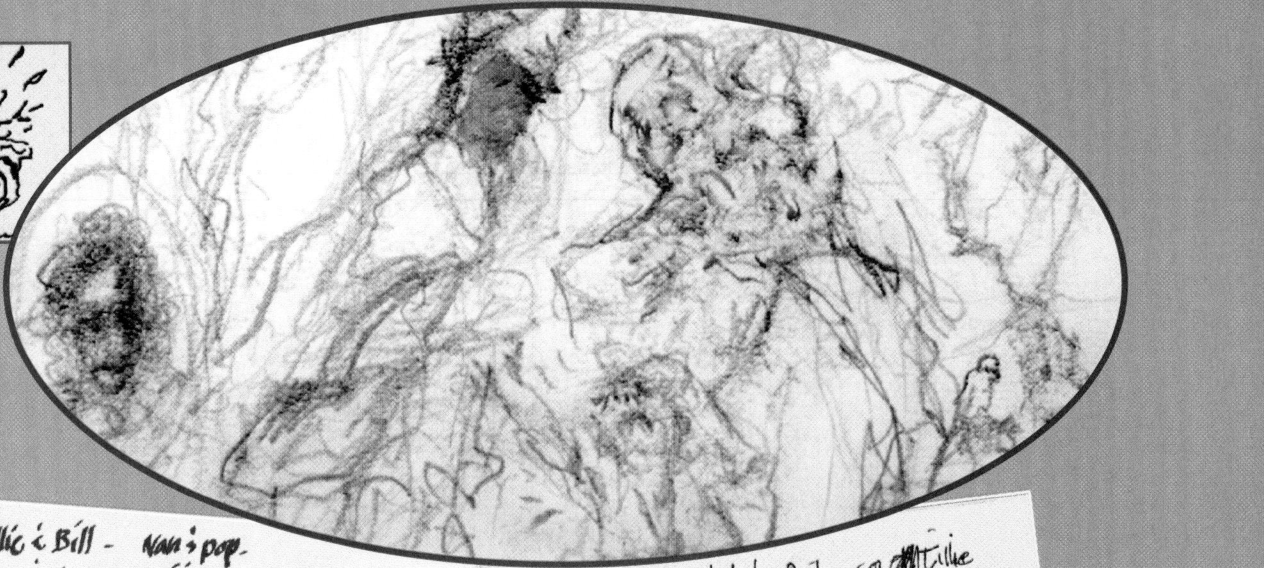

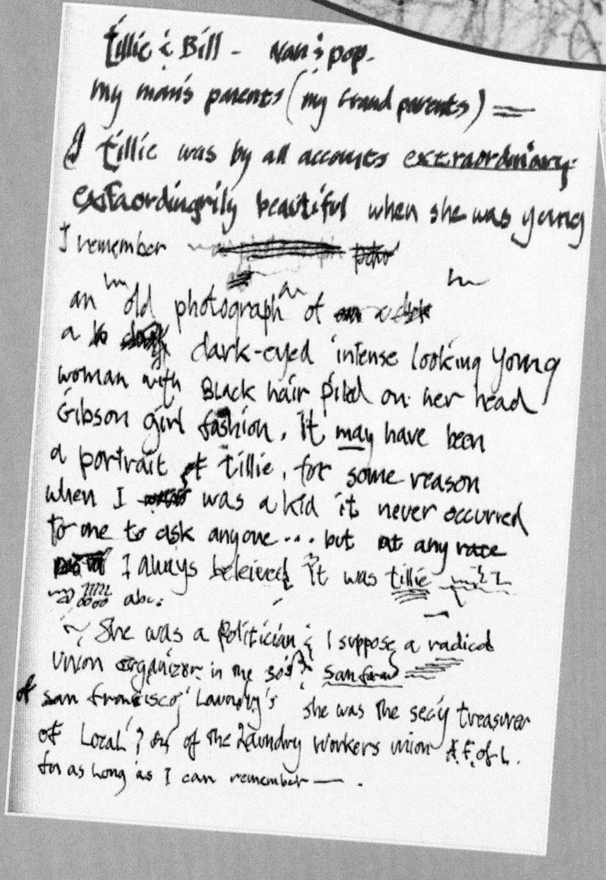

Handwritten notes (left page):

Tillie & Bill — Nan & Pop.
My mom's parents (my grand parents) =

Tillie was by all accounts ~~extraordinary~~
extraordinarily beautiful when she was young
I remember
an old photograph of
a dark-eyed intense looking young
woman with black hair piled on her head
Gibson Girl fashion. It may have been
a portrait of Tillie, for some reason
when I was a kid it never occurred
to me to ask anyone ... but at any rate
I always believed it was Tillie

She was a politician I suppose a radical
union organizer in the 30's
of San Francisco Laundry's   she was the secy treasurer
of Local ? of the Laundry Workers union A.F.of L.
for as long as I can remember

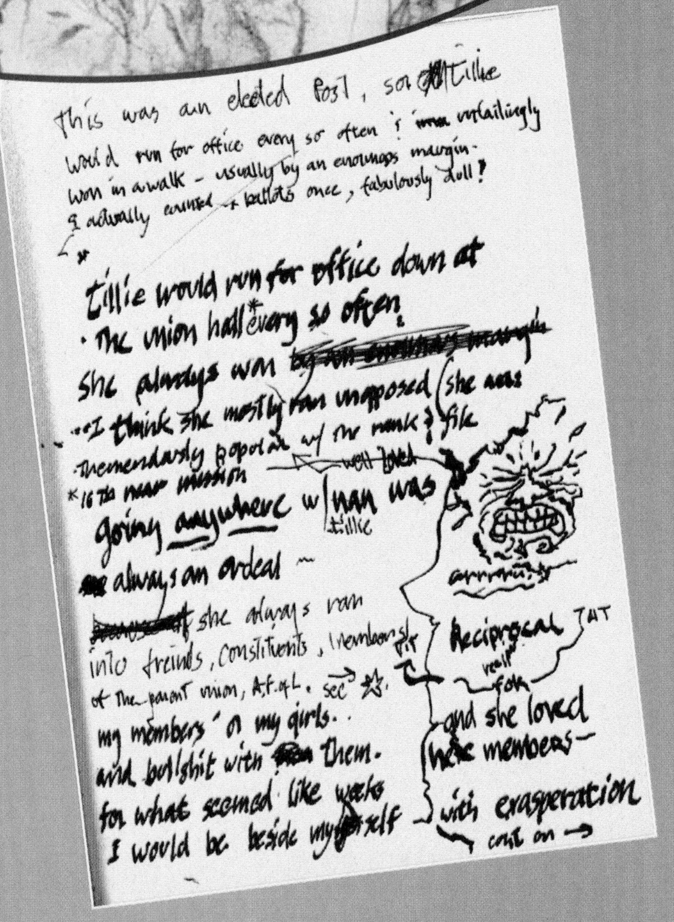

Handwritten notes (right page):

This was an elected post, so Tillie
would run for office every so often — unfailingly
won in a walk — usually by an enormous margin
& actually carried all ballots once, fabulously doll?

Tillie would run for office down at
the union hall every so often.
She always won
I think she mostly ran unopposed (she was
tremendously popular w/ the rank & file
16 to near million   well loved

going anywhere w/ Nan was
always an ordeal —
she always ran
into friends, constituents, members
of the parent union, A.F. of L. see ☆
"my members" or "my girls"
and bullshit with them.
for what seemed like weeks
I would be beside myself

Reciprocal visit
for
and she loved
these members —
with exasperation
cont on →

Tillie was by all accounts extraordinary—extraordinarily beautiful when she was young. I remember an old photograph of a dark-eyed intense-looking young woman with black hair piled on her head Gibson Girl fashion. It *may* have been a portrait of Tillie, for some reason when I was a kid it never occurred to me to ask anyone . . . but at any rate I always believed it was Tillie.

She was a politician and I suppose a radical union organizer in the 30s of San Francisco laundries. She was the secretary treasurer of Local ? of the Laundry Workers Union, A.F. of L. for as long as I can remember. This was an elected post, so Tillie would run for office down at the union hall (16th near Mission) every so often and unfailingly won in a walk—usually by an enormous margin— I actually counted ballots once, fabulously dull! She always won. I think she mostly ran unopposed. She was tremendously popular, well loved, with the rank and file. [It was reciprocal, tit for tat, and she loved her members.]

Going anywhere with Nan/Tillie was always an ordeal—she always ran into friends, constituents, members of the parent union, A.F. of L.,* "my members" or "my girls," and bullshit with them for what seemed like weeks. I would be beside myself with exasperation, seething with impatience.

"Naaaaannnn!!" I'd yell, then, with a sigh of surrender, I'd try to amuse myself, usually by "fogging" the full-length mirror by exhaling bubble-gum-flavored hot breath onto it from a distance of about one inch, or kicking those sand-filled ashtrays in what I hoped was an irritating manner, to signal (I suppose) my disapproval of these interminable hang-up schmoozings.

*San Francisco in the 40s & 50s was a union town. Harry Bridges and his longshoremen were a tremendously powerful force socially and economically, the Teamsters also—not quite up to Hoffa speed—and Harry Lundberg's Sailors Union of the Pacific (S.V.P.). The A.F. of L. was omnipresent and tremendously powerful, with a radical leftist spin.

WILLIAM HENRY
(BILL TO YOU, POP TO US)
CLIFFORD

He never spoke much at all, and that's a whole other story, see,
him and Tillie. She was a ball of fire, she was really hot. But Bill,
my grandfather, Bill Clifford, I can't imagine what drew them
together. He was So Dull. He was such a quiet person. This was
one of the Irish guys that *didn't* have the gift of gab. He couldn't tell
a story to save his soul. Or anything, I never even heard him tell a
joke. Nothin', you know, he was just a real studge, you know, he
was just yuuuuuh. Of course, I never heard him do anything bad,
either. The best story about him was that he invented the wind-
shield wiper. That's what the story was, I have no way of knowing whether he actually
did or not, you know. But — he was so dumb that he sold the patent for a thousand
dollars, which was like Big Money, you know, back in 1918, or something like that, a
thousand, or five thousand or something like that. [Maybe he was full of laughs before
then.] He might have been. I don't blame him, you know. He was like oh, jeez . . .

My grandfather used to say about the Olsen family,
my grandmother's family, that they had a drayage
business, you know, horses and carts, that sort of
thing… one of their carts had Olsen spelled with an
"O" on one side and Olsen spelled with an "E" on the
other side. My grandfather loved that — these people
were so Stupid. As far as my grandfather, who was
Irish, was concerned, it was like Stupid, they were
Stupid like Rocks, they were so dumb. He liked to
have something BAD to say about the Olsens.

Tillie was CAPTAIN OLSEN'S daughter... There's one little photograph of him, from I guess the 1880s or something like that. And he just looked so furious. He just looks mean as spit, you know, he's just an awful-lookin' guy. He's got this big forehead and a big beard grrrrrrr and these dark eyes and he just—you can't see his eyes, all you can see is shadows, you know, like an old photo, rrrrrr, and he's there in one of those naval, uh, like a pea jacket, and a captain's-type hat, you know one of those sort of vaguely . . . and long hair, and he just, he just looks . . . and everybody else in the picture is like, down here, he's like 6'5" or something, he was a huge guy.

He was born in Sweden . . . he married an Irish girl in this country, and settled down and raised a big old family, I guess. [He jumped ship, the Barbary Coast.] That's what I'm figuring . . . he jumped ship, like a lot of them did, they just abandoned their ships, left them in the harbor, they just left them there. They wanted to be in this country. And the gold thing and all that. That was a little piece of history . . .

—*Jerry Garcia's words transcribed from a taped working session for the book,
June 1995*

my ~~eahlist~~ earliest Known ancestor.

great grandfather
Capt. olsen

moms
side
Granpa
GREAT GRANDFATHER
moms mothers father
or. NANS DAD
NANS DAD

CAPTAIN OLSEN
moms granpa—
my great granpa

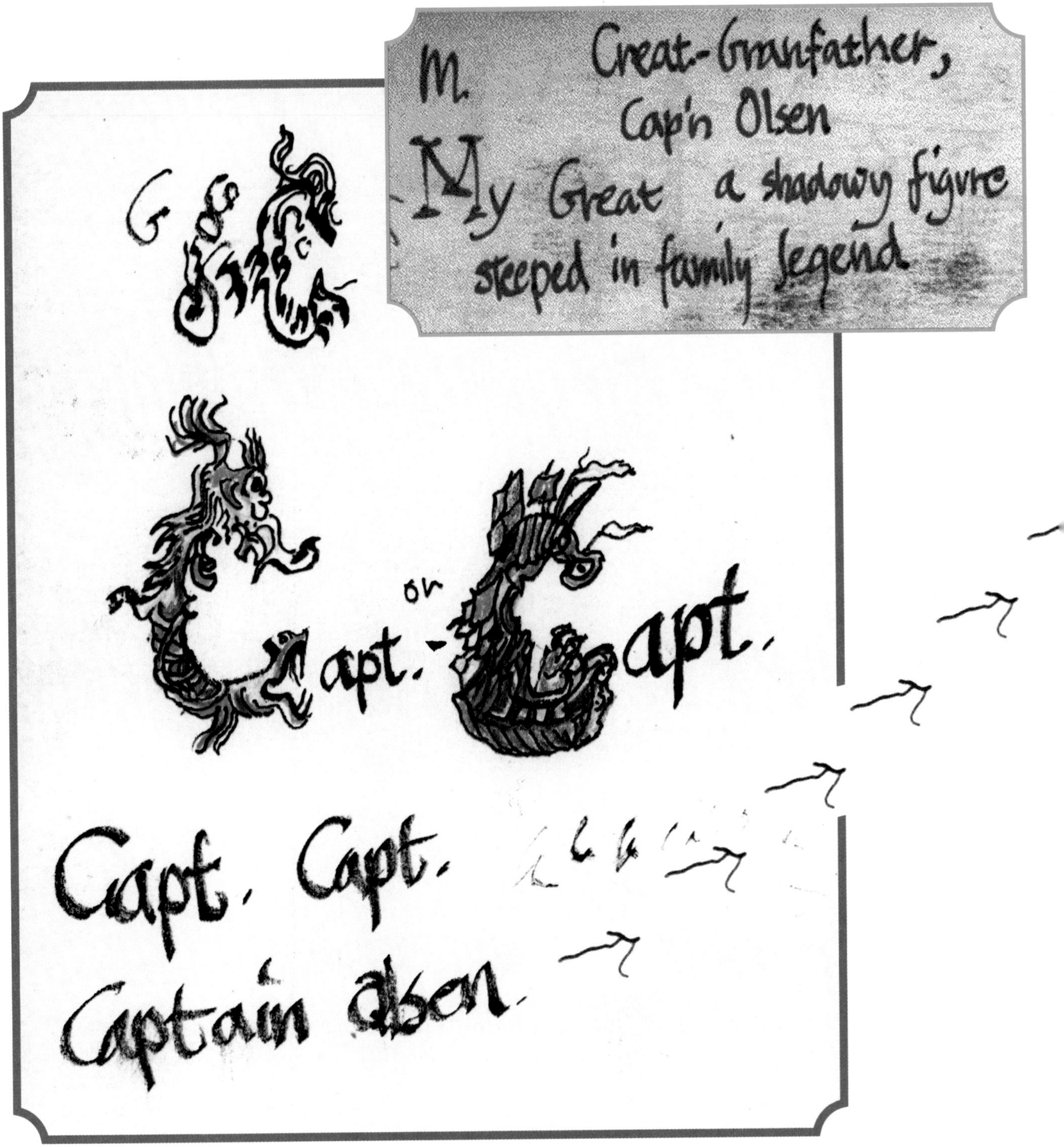

G

C

Capt. or Capt.

Capt. Capt.

Captain Olsen.

great grandfather

Is my most remote, known (to me, that is) ancestor (antecedent?). He is (was) my maternal great-grandfather and to me a shadowy, romantic figure. He was a 19th-century sea captain sailing into perilous seas from Sweden to San Francisco from the treacherous North Atlantic around the Cape of St Storms. My fantasy is he jumps ship at San Francisco and joins the hordes of fortune seekers… "The Barbary Coast"… The "early Embarcadero"… the waterfront, Russian Hill.

In truth, I only know of his existence because of a few meager pieces of evidence in the form of two anecdotes and one ancient photograph. The photograph, faded, out of focus, shows a blurred foreheady gaussian blur, as if the endless, restless motion of the sea itself had robbed from Capt. O. the ability to stand still for a photo, thereby denying the future a good look at him. Allowing him to sneak, so to speak, into the past, unseen, like the *phantom* he was…

The anecdotes go as follows:

Anecdote 1. The Captain, apparently a huge man, eschewed the use of normal bedding and regularly slept between two mattresses; you know, as though they were blankets!! This story used to fire my imagination. As a kid what I saw in my mind's eye was this giant between two immense Sealy innerspring queen-size monsters, kind of like a large swede sandwich on double box spring bread, mustard only, hold the mayo!

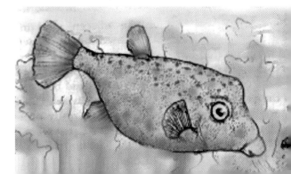

The other anecdote (#2) My grandfather (Pop) aka William Clifford used to tell with considerable relish. Although it's not about Great-Grampa Olsen specifically, it does shed some light on the nature of the Olsen clan.

The Olsen family somehow got into the cartage business, like horses, wagons, etc. Anyway one of their wagons had "OLSEN" on one side and "OLSON" on the other.

So all I know about great-grandfather Olsen was the sandwich thing, and the photograph, and the anecdote from my grandfather, that's all I know about him, then. Sleeping between the mattresses. [Kind of an archetypal figure.] Oh yeah, he must have been, if he was a sea captain, which apparently he was, he must have been one of those guys that sailed, say, from Sweden to San Francisco, around the Cape of, you know, Cape Horn, the Cape of Storms. Those were brave men, frighteningly brave. Hard, these guys. To me, he became for me when I was a kid, a mythic figure, you know what I mean? I had nothing of his to touch, you know, I didn't have anything real, only what I could come up with, what I could make up, sort of. And the photograph of him was compelling, 'cause he looked so — I mean, you could tell he didn't have the patience to stand still for it. He was already a little blurred, you know, from moving. He had a certain kind of energy that was like… he was powerful…

—*Final paragraph transcribed from June 1995 working session with Jerry Garcia*

Every morning while my brother and I were stalling to avoid going to school until the last possible minute, Pop would go through his morning routine. First he'd shave with a straight razor, stropping it furiously for a minute or two, then balancing it delicately on the sink, sharp side out.

Next he'd whip up a delicious-looking lather in his shaving cup with one of those neat shaving brushes. Finally he'd glop it on his face, scrape it neatly off with his razor, rinse and apply liberal coats of Old Spice aftershave. Then, face gleaming pinkly, he'd go (stroll) into the kitchen to continue his morning ritual (ablutions "abh loosions" yuk.). . . make coffee, the old percolator kind. Then he'd go into the little antechamber adjoining the kitchen and heading toward my grandmother's room and the back stairs.

This tiny room was the parrot's room, and he'd open the parrot's cage, insert a piece of sawed-off broomstick (we called it the "polly stick") that the parrot would eye suspiciously and maybe bite once or twice before gingerly climbing on and allowing him to place her gently on top of the cage. Then he'd give her fresh water, refill her parrot food dispenser and change the newspaper that lined her cage. Finally he'd replace her in the cage.

This routine of my grandfather's accompanied me from age five through young adulthood.

Loretta. tillies parrot

Loretta, a
brief digression:
*Never once, through
years of this daily routine,
did the parrot ever really
acknowledge Pop. But when
he died, Loretta let out a
piercing shriek, and then she
mourned him, crying like a
person until she died of grief.*

The parrot and the parrot routine virtually define "parrotness" in my life. The parrot's name was Loretta.

The story was this—immediately after the big San Francisco earthquake, with the city burning and the dust settling, my Grandma Tillie, a little girl at the time, found this parrot walking down the street!!

When my grandmother found her, she could say "prretty lorrretta." She never learned anything else speechwise, at least no more English phrases —

But she developed a perfectly wonderful vocabulary of environmental sounds, cars passing on Alemany Boulevard, faucets running, toilets flushing and her tour de force, an uncanny imitation of my grandmother's social club.

The social club was a collection of Nan's old homegirls from the 'hood who would rotate their meetings from one lady's house to another every Thursday night for an evening of cards and liquor that would get progressively more raucous as the hours passed.

The bird could do a perfectly marvelous imitation of the whole deal, cards shuffling, poker chips rattling, ice cubes clinking, old lady voices gabbling…gales of hysterical laughter.

I mean it was truly fabulous and absolutely unmistakable.

SUMMERS

we used to take auto vacations all through California and the western states. One year when I was a toddler (two or three) we were in the Santa Cruz Mountains. This may have been when my folks were shopping for our summer home. We stopped for lunch at a typical pre-war motel, you know, the kind with cabins and *no vacancy* signs and a big restaurant-cafeteria out in front and a swimming pool.

~ WATER ~

When, I was just
starting to walk
my folks, my Brother
and I were out on
a summer excursion
(we might have been
scouting for the what
eventually became
our summer cabin)
through the Santa Cruz
Mtns near Santa Cruz.
We stopped for Lunch
in Scott's valley at a
motel Lodge sort of
Restaurant deal. out
side of which

was a Typical
motel pool of that
era. (well before
the holiday Inn epoch,
close to the Bates
motel pre-war style)
you know. little cabins,
No vacancy signs etc.)
I don't remember
lunch very well
except that I had
chocolate custard
which seemed novel
to me I guess maybe
this was a wartime
thing.

I don't remember what we had for lunch but I remember chocolate custard for dessert (was it wartime rennet custard?). Anyway, after dessert I toddled outside (I may have been in a stroller, oh well) and along comes a drunk who scoops me up, exclaiming "Why hell these little bastards are just like puppies ya just throw 'em in an' they swim like fish!!" and without additional comment throws me into the pool. The deep end no less!

My Earliest Memory...

I
clearly remember
sinking majestically
to the bottom,
the soothing hush of
underwater humming
in my ears.
All in all it was
a pleasant experience.

why yes!

My father dove in and after rescuing me, he unceremoniously knocked out the drunk. Knocked him cold.

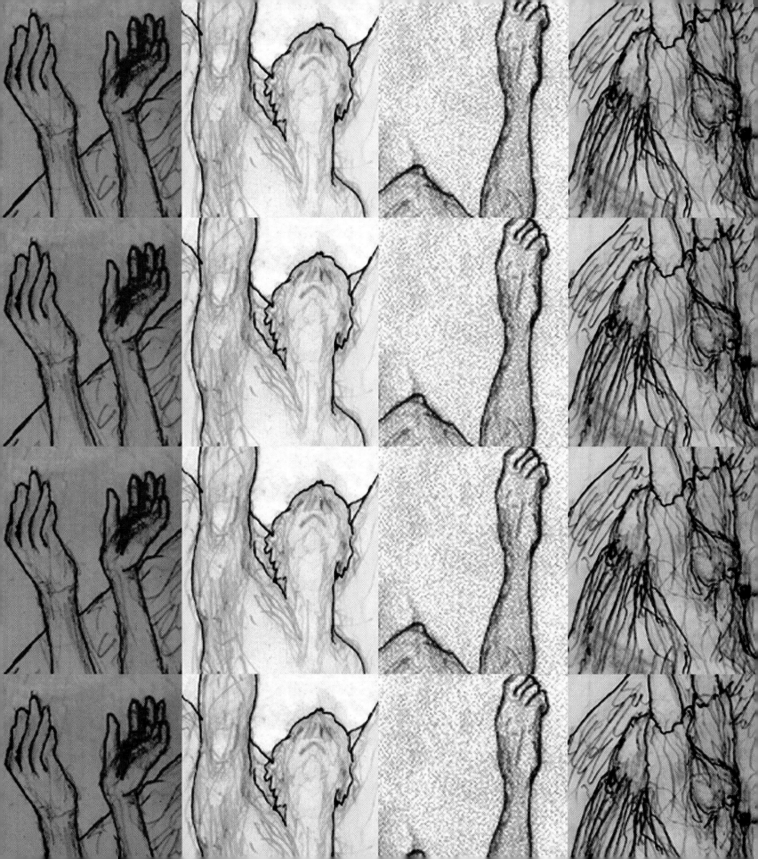

'Gods House',

'_So_, one blk., scarcely 100 yds from the door at 81 Harringt.. was 'Gods House'. In those days they still had the wonderful Latin ᚼ mass with it's, resonant sonorities and mysterious ritual movements, the incense, the music, choir, organ, Bells, candles the mured_! Light thru the stained glass windows (

My family, being mostly Irish-Spanish, was nominally Catholic, that is, the kids go to church on Sundays and holy days like Ash Wednesday, all rites and sacraments i.e.: christenings, baptisms, communions, confirmations, weddings and funerals were held under the auspices of Mother Church.

When I lived at 87 Harrington Street, the neighborhood church was Corpus Christi (body of Christ) located one block northeast of Harrington Street and occupying about one half block of area. It was, when we first moved there, a typical wooden frame, sort of classic little old church-in-the-lane cum here's the church, here's the people, open the doors, etc… kind of deal.

It was part of a larger complex including convent, primary school, residences for priests and nuns, chapels… Like I said, about half-a-block area in all.

Anyway, in 1949 they tore the whole complex down and started building an ultramodern, no crosses, no statuary, no steeple, rectangular bauhaus kind of nontraditional church. This transformation was occurring throughout the diocese, and strange modern churches were springing, like weird mutant mushrooms, up all over the place.

As I recall it, the parishioners at the time were not very happy with these angular, bizarre, clearly nontraditional, possibly even heretic intruders into the familiar forms and wholesome shapes that represent God's House, Mother Church, supportive, nurturing, gathering the community in…

an aside:

These "modern" churches were hailed in architectural journals and other elitist media as the Church's return to the cutting edge of patronage, a position it had not occupied since right around the Renaissance.

 The Excelsior district of San Fransisco was ethnically mostly Italian and Irish. My family was pretty much Spanish-Irish, a stricken combination of Catholicism's Weirder Interpretations. Luckily my mother's side of the family had an iconoclastic approach—probably the union stuff—to religion so we kids were given our collection money and spruced up on Sunday morning and sent to the eight o'clock Mass and of course catechism. For non-Catholics this stuff was an impenetrable bramble of bizarre dogma, perfectly calculated to encase the seven-year-old intellect in moral concrete.

I remember worrying, with all the pious sincerity I could muster, should I happen upon a fatally wounded pagan would I have the presence of mind to correctly administer a baptism before seeking medical aid so as to ensure the survival of his/her immortal soul! Whew!

So, one block, scarcely 100 yards from the door at 87 Harrington, was God's House! In those days they still had the wonderful Latin Mass with its resonant sonorities and mysterious ritual movements, the incense, the music, choir, organ, bells, candles, the muted light through the stained glass windows.

The whole thing was deliciously scary. and of course properly inspirational. It was this sure-fire environment. not so effectively misinforming my own muddled sense of the numinous and crippled me with.

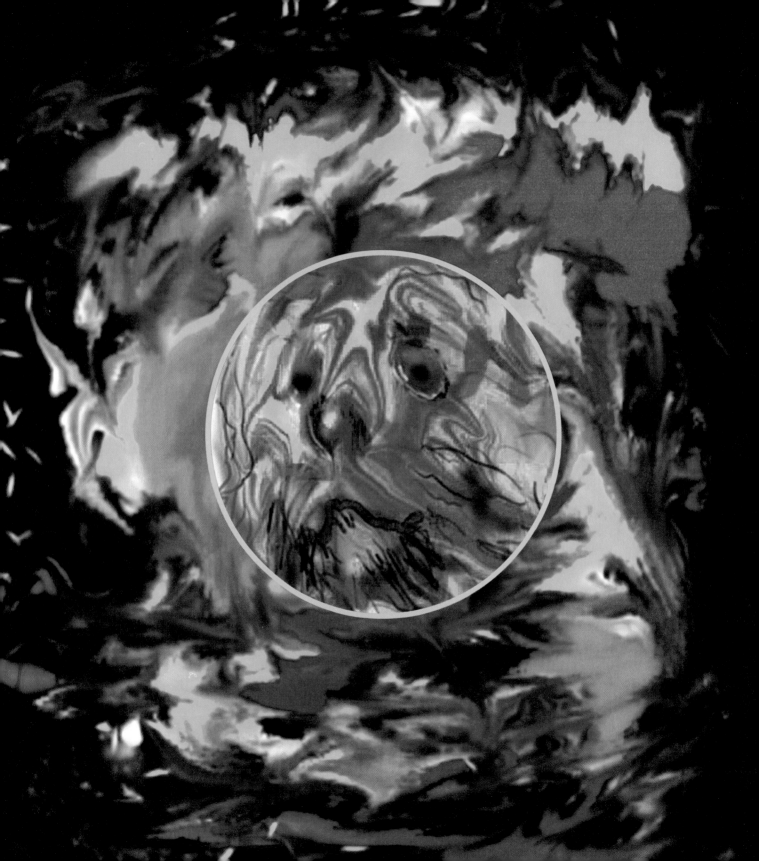

Jerry used to walk home from school every day. One day he saw
two PIERCING eyes looking at him through the leaves of a

ush. He thought it was a cat and he bent down and said

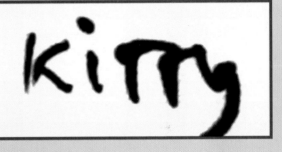

and a BIG RAT

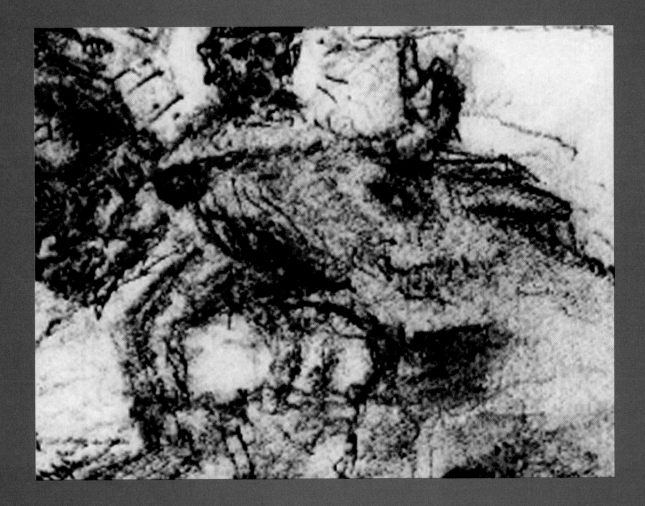

jumped out

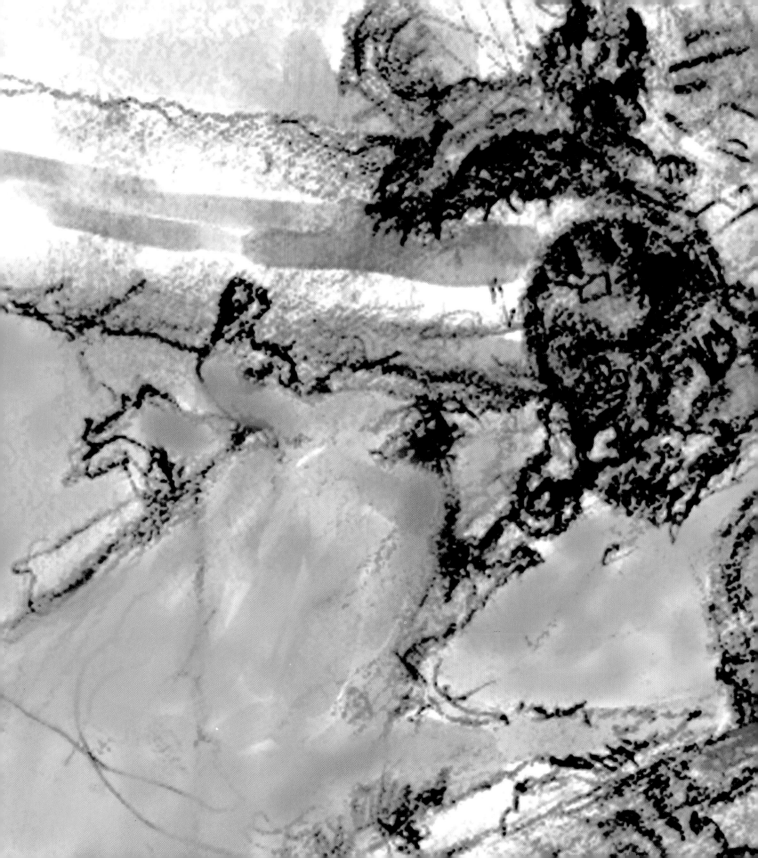

and he RAN . . .

like hell all the way home...

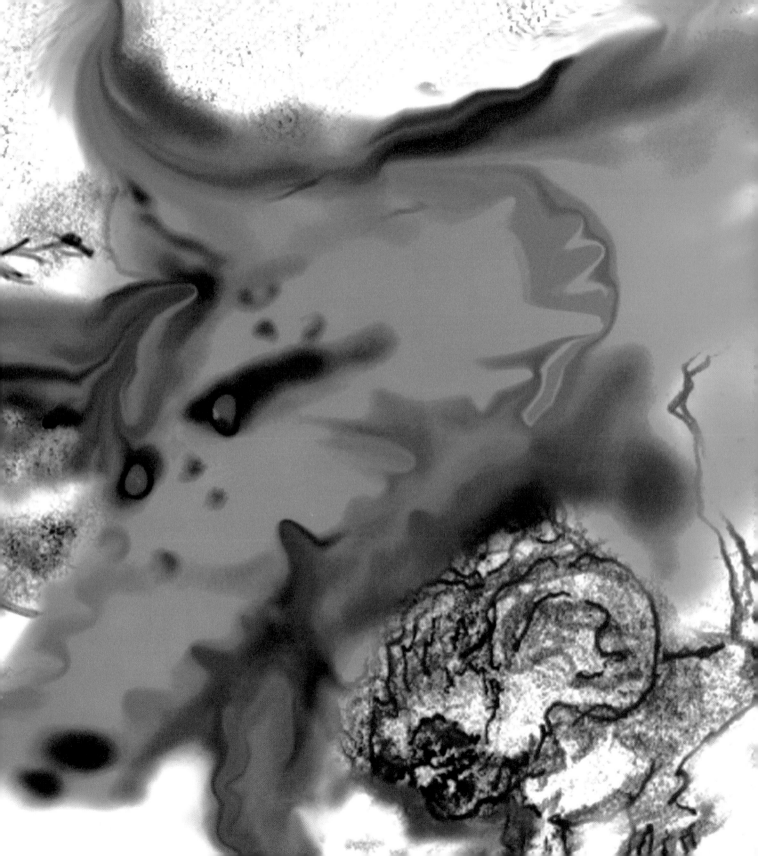

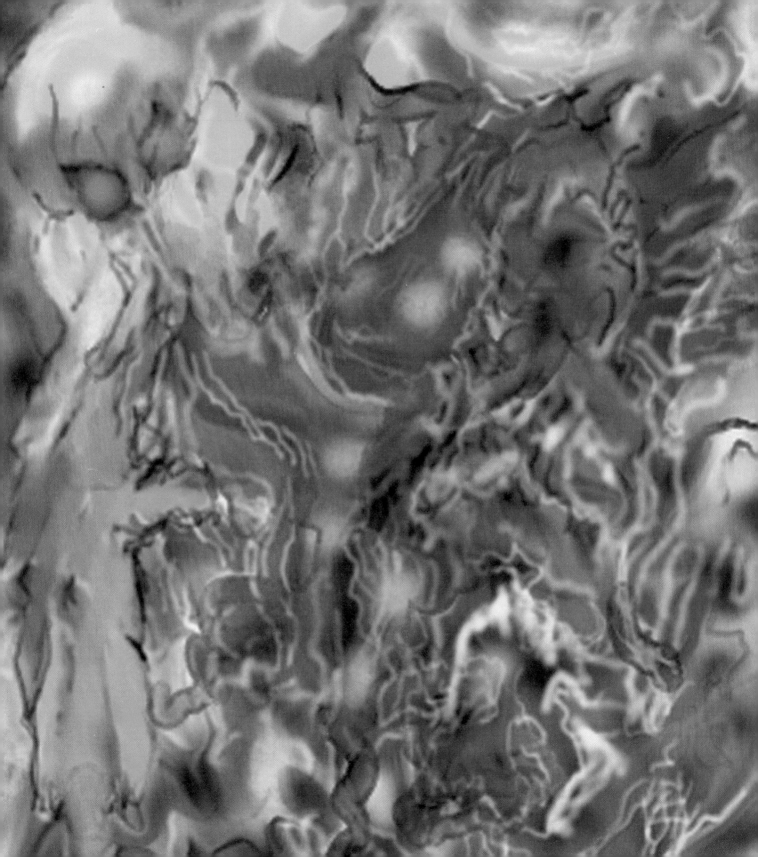

to Harrington Street...
where Nan would let him climb into bed with her
when his **Lucid Nightmares** *became too real...*

For me one of the most intense "alpha" discoveries & power-acquisition rituals was…

… Or, if you prefer the colloquial variant, playing with matches!

My family had a summer cabin in the Santa Cruz Mountains. Every night when we finished dinner we'd have a sort of campfire and sometimes us kids would get to roast marshmallows (under adult supervision of course).

This was the first step in the Playing with Fire chapter. I admit we weren't truly allowed to P.W.F. [play with fire] but after the third bag of marshmallows and the 30th chorus of "Maryann McCarthy she went out to dig some clams," the adult supervision mode slowly slid into the benign neglect mode and we kids were able to …

The marshmallows' primary role slowly devolved from confectionery treats to blazing torches!

The amazing seductive power of a one-on-one relationship with the elemental destructor, living, breathing, actively devouring everything in its path. True Power corrupting little me, transforming me into a wet-eyed pyromaniac, the high-frequency buzz of a fine Lunacy drowning out the fire alarms and screaming hook-and-ladders summoned to the blaze.

playing with fire

playing with fire

playing with fire

I think it started with …

Roasting Marshmallows—

over the campfire, after the 6th or 7th marshmallow had been cremated and devoured

(I always tried to achieve a uniform "golden brown" exterior but they always seemed

to burst into flame and ended up as crinkly chunks of carbon) and the pointed end of

the stick was poised near enough to the flame so that ever so slowly the end of the

stick would catch fire!

Usually the adults would be lulled by Marshmallow Lethargy into a state of

non-watchfulness.

This was the moment when I was finally able to play

(in a semi-supervised way)

with fire.

What a marvelous adventure

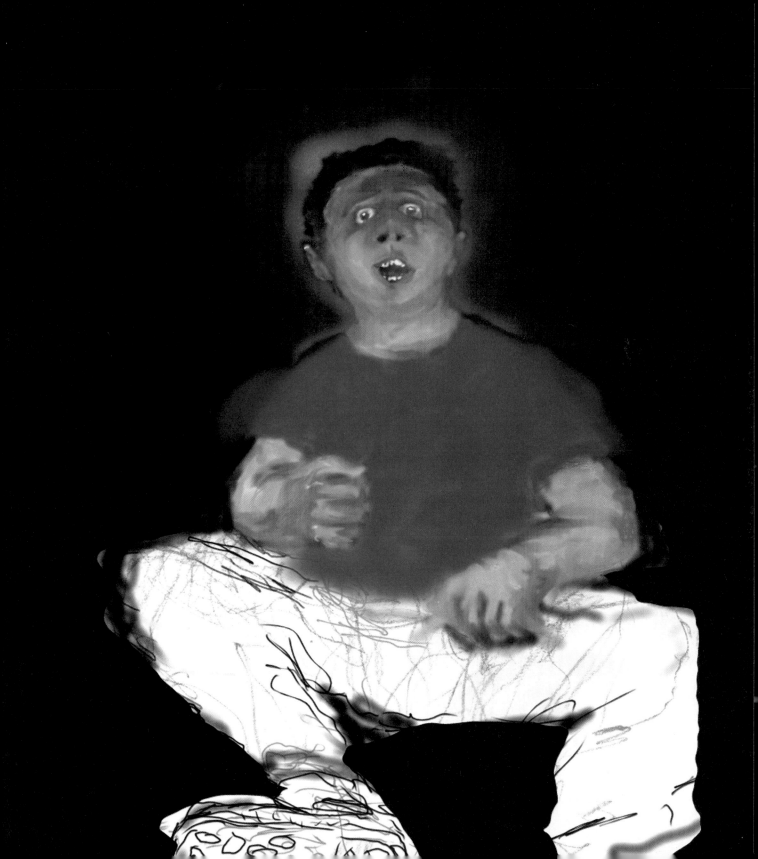

Girls up the street

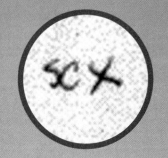

When he was very young, the girls
up the street, mean girls, would
corner him, make him stand on a
box and take his pants down. They
would look at him and laugh.
It was horrible…

After drawing it and thinking about it
all these years later, Jerry laughed.

and this is as much as he told us…

"me"